SKELETONS IN THE CLOSET

Memoirs of a Pastor's Son.

2nd Edition.

✓ Revised.
✓ Corrected.
✓ Improved.
✓ Expanded.
✓ Renewed.

Alias Martín García

SKELETONS IN THE CLOSET - MEMOIRS OF A PASTOR'S SON - 2ND EDITION

First edition. October 31, 2023.

ISBN: 979-8223864493

Written by Alias Martín Garcia.

Also by Alias Martín Garcia

SKELETONS IN THE CLOSET: Memories of a Son of a Pastor
Esqueletos en el Closet - Memorias de un hijo de Pastor - 2da Edición
Skeletons in the Closet - Memoirs of a Pastor's Son - 2nd Edition

Skeletons in the Closet: Memoirs of a Pastor's Son.

2nd. Edition.

Revised.
Corrected.
Improved.

Expanded.
Renewed.

Cover design created from images generated by:
https://stablediffusionweb.com and some free web resources.
ALIAS MARTÍN GARCÍA
2023

DEDICATION

I dedicate this book to leaders and pastors, to the children of pastors around the world and to my 5 brothers for whom I pray every day to be saved.

CONTENT

INTRODUCTION

The children of pastors and leaders often have to mature faster than the rest of the people in the church because the environment in which we develop is more mature, even though our parents want to take care of these things for us, many of us from a very young age are afraid. You have to be part of situations and hear conversations daily that a common Christian would find difficult to digest.

In some cases, these experiences cause some pastors' children to abandon the path of the gospel, others become very cold and only learn the ways and means and they are in the gospel, but the gospel is not in them.

When making the decision to write these memoirs or this summary of my memoirs, the questions never cease: Is it to avoid having to pay a psychologist? What teaching or how can this book be a blessing to those who read it?

While I was writing the first manuscript, the answers to those questions were answering themselves and I hope you can easily notice it. In any case, in each chapter I do not stop repeating the reasons why I decided to write this book so that my motivations and intentions are not misinterpreted.

I would like you to keep in mind before starting to read this book that there is at least one more book on the market that deals with the topic of pastors' children, written by Barnabas Piper, son of Pastor John Pipper and I thought it was super cute.

I don't find it reasonable to write another book dealing with the same things. If you want to read something nice, I recommend that book. The truth is, what I describe in this book is not all nice, but it can be a great blessing if you look at it correctly.

A video of a car crash might look simply horrifying, but a good observer could learn a lot from the crash so that it doesn't happen to them.

I believe that this book or these memoirs can help pastors and leaders to reconsider how to choose leadership and how to teach and help those they intend to appoint as leaders. Mainly to see a little beyond the talents. I remember something that I witnessed very closely where a person who stole cars was converted and a few months later he was named pastor because he had certain gifts, but this man still continued to steal cars. And the pastors brag to others "what God did" that with just six months a former thief is already a pastor. Moses spent 40 years being prosecuted. Why do we have to pursue this "microwave" madness?

I think this book could also help church members from making the same mistakes that the church members in the final chapters made that contributed to the pastor this book refers to having a closet full of skeletons. Sometimes church members are directly to blame for a pastor's harm, which is the case recounted in this book.

I am sure that this book will also be of help to the children of pastors from a pastor's son who by grace did not depart and did not decide to navigate within the church just learning how this world of ministry moves. Let me explain, among the children of pastors, in my opinion there are 4 groups:

1. Those who remain firm in the gospel.

2. Those who separate themselves due to different things they saw in the same family.

3. Those who simply wanted nothing to do with the gospel.

4. They saw many horrible things in the family, with their parents being pastors, but they continue in the gospel only because they learned the mechanics of how everything moves in the ministry and they probably ended up replicating the same gospel that they saw in their home where they lived. He preaches one thing, but lives another.

I believe that this book could help all 4 groups. I personally believe that the worst of the 4 groups is number 4 because it usually happens with many children of pastors who do not have any kind of communion with God, but they learned how this whole world of ministry moves and I am more concerned about this group because they They believe they are Christians because they attend all the services, they even teach others, they give teachings but only because they learned the mechanics and they know what a prayer is like that the majority accepts as correct, they know what a preaching is like that people accept as correct while they are totally separated from God. I hope this book contributes a lot to group number 4.

This book is not to save me a psychologist or to release hatred or resentments. My greatest hope is that this book helps leaders, pastors, and children of pastors.

To date, the majority of my brothers, all raised in the world of the church and with extensive biblical knowledge, are outside the gospel because they saw and lived incomprehensible things that occur within some ministry families and they did not have the necessary help.

I hope with these memoirs that leaders, pastors and church members open their understanding in many aspects and have spiritual eyes open to help people whose parents could see themselves as the most qualified ministers in the world, but who have closets full of skeletons in their homes. .

In this book, to protect people's privacy, I will not give real names of any person or ministry. I myself have decided not to give my name and therefore from the cover to the end I will refer to myself as Alias Martin García, but I assure you before God that every word of what I write is totally true.

In this second edition in its three versions, e-book, physical and audio book, I have added extra material where the veracity of what I say is shown a little without exposing myself to revealing any identity.

As I will repeat several times in this book, my idea is to leave a message and not expose all the errors or failures of people, that is why I will only mention a certain small number of events, those that

I consider necessary so that the message I want to leave can be understood.

CHAPTER 1
Contextualizing: History before stories.

I am Alias Martin García and this is the story before the stories.

I consider it important to place this chapter because this chapter and in general the first chapters provide the context to be able to understand the reasons that led to the occurrence of situations that I will mention later.

I am the 2nd of 6 siblings, two girls and 4 boys, my parents: a man born in the interior of a country in America and a woman born on an English-speaking island in the Caribbean.

My grandmother moved to this country with my mother's stepfather, who mistreated her a lot and in her desperation for an escape, she agreed to my father's demands and took her to live with his family.

My father, an alcoholic and smoker, did not know any trade and did not even have an education; my mother had barely finished basic education. My father's job was to scam people by playing cards.

Unfortunately, my father was not a sweetheart and this lack of affection that my mother had will work against her later.

Their beginning of life as a couple was hell, because the abuse from my father's family was immediate as they denigrated my mother for being black, although she is not really black but rather dark like anyone in this American country where she lives. But, such immoral Indians the color of an overcooked coffee bean had the pretensions to mistreat my mother for being black, although I rather believe that they did not call her black because of her color but because she was a descendant of blacks.

They seemed to have all the ingredients for failure. Let the betting begin! How many months do we give this pair?

My mother tells me that the situation with my parents' family was so strong that she felt like she was going crazy, so much so that one time they went out to look for a house to buy without having a single coin in their pocket.

In the end they ended up at my maternal grandmother who gave them land with a mud house where my own memories of those times really begin.

In this mud house that, as they say around here, when it rained it got wetter inside than outside, we spent our first period of hunger, and by then there were three of us, the first three men.

I have very interesting memories of that time. I remember neighbors giving us two plates of food for 5 and my parents giving them to us while they were starving. I also remember an aunt's fights with my grandmother. When my grandmother wanted to pass us a plate of food, my aunt yelled at her: Are you going to give my food to those starving people?!

I also remember my first experience with demonized people because from that young age we had to see my aunt (yes, the same one who prevented my grandmother from giving us food while we were hungry, it couldn't be anyone else-) being possessed by demons, both that changed shape.

Conversion of my parents and first steps in the Gospel

In the midst of all this the conversion of my parents occurred. They tell me that in a campaign of the Pentecostal brothers the preacher cried out asking who was the brave man who wanted to come to receive Christ and my father, in the middle of a drunken state that could not even stand, answered "I am brave" and passed. He says that at the same moment his drunkenness lifted and his first steps in the gospel began.

He says that he had no problems quitting smoking, it was instantaneous, but the temptation for liquor was horrible.

He relates that he was once returning from a church service and one of his old party friends showed him a beer and said, "Come drink one." He says that he came home troubled, desperate because the image of that delicious bottle of cold beer kept repeating in his mind. He told us that at that moment he knelt down and cried out to God and said:

"If you don't take away this desire, I'm going to go get that beer" and at that moment God took away that desire for liquor forever.

My father grew up in the gospel and began to be taken into account as a preacher, my mother began to be part of the praise group and was the designated worship director. It is good to understand from this chapter that at that time the praise groups of the Pentecostal churches were not very organized nor did they seek excellence because "God cares about what matters to the heart."

Already at this time our life had changed, my father went from scamming people with card games to being a serious, responsible worker and supplier for his family. He then started working in an oil company as a simple assistant, but with the wisdom and grace that only God gives, he became a crew leader.

Ministerial growth continued for both of us, my mother little by little began to become a Bible scholar and also to be known as a rebel for not accepting any doctrine that did not have a biblical basis and as we all know, no pastor likes this type of people. and they always ended up calling them arrogant and rebellious. Every shepherd loves submissives. Unfortunately, she would end up doing the same much later. But let's not get ahead of ourselves, let's go step by step.

CHAPTER 2
One and another and another.

The very fact that my parents did not accept extra-biblical or anti-biblical doctrines caused them to be expelled from several churches and they simply left others themselves. I think that by the time I was 10 years old we had already gone through 5 different congregations And those that were missing!

We passed by a congregation where the pastor had a love life with the prophet of the church and they even had a child, we passed by another church where the pastor had a love life with one of the worshipers, by one where they were called "the quiet ones" we passed by others who had such strange doctrines that I am sure they were sects.

Me too? Why don't I show up yet?

Well, since I was little, my parents always had me and my other two male brothers give special performances by singing a song of praise or worship in Pentecostal campaigns, which is why I practically grew up with a microphone in hand.

I particularly loved singing, my younger brother loved the drums and the guitar and the oldest, well, the oldest of my brothers loved the girls, and no, I'm not talking about the small guitars but the girls from the church.

CHAPTER 3
This is the One.

It was the nineties, the last church where we had been was a false doctrine, almost a cult, and the last straw was that the pastor was unfaithful to his wife and we couldn't stay there. They were quiet, but terrible.

My parents were already disappointed in everything called a pastor and anything called a church. Many times people had prophesied to my father that he would be a pastor, but he understood that it was not yet time.

In many conversations my parents only repeated the phrase "If God calls us to the pastorate, we will not do any of those bad things that we have seen pastors do." Above all, they referred to deception, manipulation, mistreatment, or attacking those who do not agree. with them or abuse their power as pastors. While we children heard this phrase, I for my part was happy and waited for that moment when they would be shepherds, trusting that they would never do the ugly things that I saw others doing.

At one point someone told my parents about a new group that was gathering with a couple of newly married engineers who came from the central plains of the country, my parents went and they thought it was very good.

We children thought it was cool. They worked with mimes, plays and choreography and for us that whole form of evangelism was something new and wonderful. Furthermore, they had the intelligence and sagacity to add us to all the groups quickly.

For a few years we lived in special times, a new man in the pastorate who was a better pastor than all the experienced pastors we had known and an even better pastor than he himself is today. They were almost magical years.

There I met a worship leader who would change my life, received my first official education in music, and took my first steps as a worship leader.

That rookie pastor had a discipline that was horrendous, but that I loved; I remember that those of us who chose to be part of the praise group had to take a 6-month preparation that included singing classes, demonstrate fidelity to God by not failing any of the services or rehearsals or any church activity, and Our family members had to attest that we had good behavior and a life of communion with God.

Apart from that, we were called to be the first to arrive at the church and if the pastor arrived at the church and saw the church dirty or chairs out of place or water on the floor and we are there and we had not fixed it, it was certain that the pastor would tell us. He scolded because the idea was to take away that elitist spirit that those in the praise group usually have and teach us to be servants instead of always seeking to be served, which is one of the great problems of the members of the praise groups to this day. .

I always remember one Sunday morning that, as always, all of us who were opting to be part of the praise group arrived early and we were joking for a while and we heard the sound of that red Corolla! and we looked out the window and it was the shepherd!

What is the shepherd doing here so early?! We all wondered and quickly looked everywhere in the church to see if there was anything dirty or messy and it turns out that there was some water spilled on the floor and one of the most delicate girls just that day had worn a beautiful dress and ran, He took a cloth and got down on his knees and wiped away that water.

In truth it was not because of fear of the pastor, because in truth we all loved him, for years whenever I spoke and told about him, I referred to him as the best pastor I had ever met, until a few months ago I heard from him again and I discovered that he crossed over to the dark side, he crossed over to the side of the heretics who sacrifice the truth of the gospel to have large numbers of people in the church.

I have another "nice" memory from those times and it has to do with me. At that time, one of the rules for those of us who chose to be part of the praise group was that we did not have to miss rehearsals and stay at rehearsals until they were over, but the praise leader usually arrived late to Saturday rehearsals. and rehearsals often ended at midnight. Thank God I had an uncle who was already part of the praise team and took me home.

It had been several Saturdays since I arrived home at 12:15 at night and my mother was not very happy with that and told me "You come back at 12 at night and sleep on the platform."

That following Saturday after my mother gave me the "ultimatum" The leader of the praise group arrived late as always and in the middle of the rehearsal as the hours passed, I just looked at the clock until it was 12 midnight and then I had peace because I told myself "No way, I have to sleep outside"

My mother, who I always loved for that way of being, for doing what she said, when I got home I found the door closed and it was no use knocking, so I got on the platform as best I could and lay down as best I could on the concrete. , and thank God I was able to sleep, although in the morning I had to remove, with great pain, small pebbles that were stuck to my skin due to sleeping on the concrete.

Today, as I write this, I think about the thoughtlessness of the worship team leader, but at the time it was the price I had to pay for my dream of being part of the praise team and I gladly endured it.

They are marks that I carry without weight or pain, especially when today those in praise groups are not taught to be disciplined, they do not pay the price for anything, they are not taught to be servants and I think that is precisely why they have that elitist spirit. Over the years I don't know if I met a member of a worship group who didn't have that elitist spirit.

The sad thing is that current pastors no longer form people like that. For them it is enough that the musicians play, the singers sing and that's it. I remember one time trying to teach that type of discipline, obviously not finishing rehearsals at 12 at night, that is honestly abuse, and when trying to teach that type of discipline the pastors destroyed me, a pastor told me "What I want is that you teach them to sing, nothing more"

A few months ago, I visited that church and the worship team is in ruins. But that story comes later when we start to see the skeletons inside the closet.

Well, everything was going perfectly well in that church, the church began to grow exponentially... But, but suddenly everything began to go perfectly wrong.

And everything began to go perfectly wrong, not because of the reduction in the number of people in the church, because the truth is that for a while there were more of us every day, but at a certain moment it was determined that since the church was started by young people and young people, they were the ones who brought people to the church with their type of evangelism, so they had to be given freedom. Serious mistake! Young people began to be allowed practically everything.

Suddenly the "Apostle" of that ministry... Oh, time for an explanatory parenthesis! Well, I hadn't mentioned that. That ministry had what was new for us at that time, The Apostles! People who had not seen Jesus, which is one of the requirements to be an apostle, but who call themselves apostles. It comes to mind that a few days ago a pastor explained that they told him "But they say they are Apostles" and he says that he responded "There are people out there who say they are Napoleon and that does not mean that they are Napoleon."

At that time, the early 90s, the apostles thing was quite new, not like now when they even come in McDonald's boxes. There are even places where you take a course for a few months and they give you an apostle certificate.

For my part, I always say that I do not deny that apostles can exist, but first I must see that they fulfill the functions that the first apostles had and until now I have not seen any do so. The only thing they do is "confirm the believers" who, by the way, each one has their own interpretation of what that means, but meeting to put order in the church as the true apostles did, never! just confirm.

Having briefly explained what refers to the apostles, I continue with the story. The truth is that for reasons that have nothing to do with the purpose of this book, the apostle of that ministry removed our pastor and began to change our pastor as if it were underwear and each one surpassed the previous one in how bad they were. was.

They all had the same characteristics: They wanted everyone to like them, some had charisma, others just struggled to be liked, I imagine so they wouldn't be removed like the others, but in the end none of them worked as well as the first.

CHAPTER 4
One Worse than the Other.

I remember that the next pastor we were appointed to had a couple of daughters whom he placed as youth and praise group leaders along with their boyfriends. At that time we were still congregating in the meeting room of a hotel in the city.

These beautiful daughters of the pastor and leaders of the youth and the praise group, at the end of the Saturday praise rehearsal, went to hang out at a club that was half a block from the hotel. Nobody told us about it, two of my brothers and I saw it with our own eyes and not once, not twice, not three times, but repeatedly and no, it wasn't to buy ice or bottles of mineral water.

Linda my mother, when we told her what we had discovered that our new leaders were doing, she taught us that we should not disrespect our leaders, but that whatever they did, we should respect them as leaders.

Then it became widely known that these girls and their boyfriends practiced a type of gospel that was not yet well known in the city where we lived, a gospel where the world and the church mix and the difference ends up being lost.

On another occasion, going to a camp for church youth, the kind they used to do in those days, we were traveling on the bus, I was sitting in one of the middle seats and I see that those in front ask me to pass a cooler to the back and then the people in the back asked me to return them to the people in front, this happened so many times that I got tired and I opened the cooler and to my amazement what was in the cooler was rum! It's been more than twenty years and it still surprises me. Some young people traveling to a Christian camp were drinking RON!

By this time my father was already a leader in the church, strong in his word. strong in prayer, recognized and loved and with the fastest growing cell in the church.

But at home it was a quite different story, at home he was not that example and effective leader. At home it was very horrible, my older brother, my younger brother and I tried to seek help from the pastor, the pastor did not give us the benefit of the doubt, he spoke to our father and things got worse.

I was the last one to ask the pastor for help and what happened as a result of talking to that pastor would mark me for life. The pastor told everything to my father, my father told him that I was demon-possessed and I found out that one night the pastor came to the house "to get the demons out of me."

While that pastor shouted, rebuking my demons, I just looked at him with tears in my eyes, because I trusted him by telling him our situation and instead of giving us the benefit of the doubt and at least praying and investigating how he was a new pastor, he preferred to find a way to ingratiate himself with one of the most prominent leaders like my father was at that time.

They kept shouting, rebuking me "to the devil" and I just continued looking at the pastor and crying. After a while, as I saw that they did not stop rebuking the devil, I moved my hands abruptly and fell to the floor while the pastor shouted with joy because the supposed demon had come out.

Never again did any of the three brothers have the confidence to tell the family situation to another pastor.

Returning to the topic of the church, it turns out that what began as something beautiful, like the congregation of our dreams, was beginning to turn into a nightmare.

Then the apostle appointed another pastor. By then we were continuing to grow in quantity, but declining in quality. Since the hotel's meeting room had become too small, a fairly large room was rented even though the previous pastor was there. At that time we became the largest church in the city.

In the midst of so much crazy stuff in the church, I mean we had a lot of people, but in terms of Christianity perhaps we were the worst church, but in the midst of that I as a worshiper was growing. I had been part of the church choir for years, I was in the back row, I never dreamed of being a worship director because I hated my voice, but I loved singing to God, it's strange, but that's how it was and with my love for singing to Him, I had designed certain strategies to force myself to give fresh worship to God.

By that time God had already blessed my parents greatly, and my dad went from working at the oil company and set up a car painting workshop in the yard of a house that he bought from my grandparents and through the pure goodness of God it was possible. build a three-story house.

I used to go to the third floor of the house and start singing songs for a while and then I would say to myself "Well, that's what whoever wrote that song wanted to tell God, now use the same melodies and tell Him something." your own heart" sometimes it was difficult for me, but by doing it continuously I began to have beautiful moments of genuine adoration of God.

Over time, interesting things began to happen, sometimes I was watching a movie with my family or simply there with them, which was not normal because I was very withdrawn, I did not usually interact much and being like this I felt within me a call to go away to worship him, to be with him. Sometimes he would say, "Don't be religious, you hardly spend time with your family and when you're with them for a while, are you going to leave?", but in the end I always left because I loved spending time with him.

Many years before the situation had occurred that I heard my mother pray at dawn and I was shocked by her way of praying, so I asked her to teach me to pray like her and the very tremendous one told me "I'm going to get you up once, then you get up on your own"

I was about thirteen years old and she was praying at 2 in the morning and she told me "I'm going to get you up just once" tremendously my mother. The truth is that at the beginning it was very strong, it didn't last even 5 minutes and she prayed from 2 in the morning to 6 in the morning, that is, she prayed for 4 hours and I had no more and no less than 3 hours and 55 minutes left over.

She instructed me, telling me to first repeat what she prayed, then after a few days praying the same thing she prayed, to little by little add my words until the prayer became totally mine. After a few months, a 13-year-old teenager was already praying for 4 hours and not religiously, but it was a delight.

And since with the experience I had with my mother in prayer I had already practiced what it was like to be in the presence of God, what I did in worship on the third floor of the house was to find new delightful ways to be in his presence.

As I already explained, in the praise group I felt comfortable being in the back row of the choir, no one ever saw me, my voice was never heard and the truth is that I didn't care, I was extremely introverted and on top of that I didn't like my voice like that. that I had no problem with the fact that they did not see or hear me, until one day I felt the presence of the holy spirit so strongly in the middle of worship and the whole church heard my voice and I could neither lower my voice nor remain silent. until it finished.

Everyone was surprised and I think I was more so. After that, an uncle of mine, who was at that time the leader of the praise group, decided to start making me sing worship alone on Sundays and accompanied by another person because of my introversion problems.

He sang glued to the microphone without moving, but I didn't need anything else, the glory of God filled the place as I began to sing. I lasted like this for a few years without problem. I loved the praise group, I loved worshiping him, even if he was in the last place in the choir line as he was before.

After about two years or so, one of the grayest moments in my ministerial life happened. Some brothers from the church helped me by paying my registration and monthly fees to study in a technological school and I could not attend the three rehearsals that the praise group had, because I was in classes and according to what they told me later, the devil had sown envy in the heart of some of those in the praise group because they praised so much how the presence of God moved while I led.

The truth is that they went to my place of study and told me that I have to go to an urgent meeting of the praise group, I go with them and when I get to the church the meeting was only with me and it surprised me. Then, two of my uncles and others from the praise group meet, and they tell me that the meeting is to inform me that because I couldn't be in two of the three praise group rehearsals, I couldn't continue being part of it.

The sky fell, my heart broke and especially because some of those who were doing that to me were my family. I asked to speak and told them all the sacrifice and dedication that I had had in the praise group, something that none of them had ever done.

At that moment in the initial praise group where I started, there was only one of my uncles and me left. None of them had paid the price I paid. After I said what I had to say, I asked one of my uncles to take me home and there I cried bitterly.

My mother was more aware than I of why everything happened. She gave me a great lesson, she told me "You from your seat, worshiping as you have always done, are going to show her that you are a true worshiper." And so I did, without seeking to prove anything, just being and doing what I he already did in secret.

CHAPTER 5
The tower of cards falls.

Suddenly the largest church in the city began to become desolate and there was no longer enough to pay for such a place and we had to start holding services in the parking lot of a house belonging to one of the sisters who congregated at the church.

Before we moved to congregate in the parking lot of the sister's house, another new pastor had been announced, so we came to congregate in the parking lot with a new pastor. The guy was charismatic, as a new boss he wanted everyone to like him, he was able to impress among the young people because we already knew him from seeing him at the youth and dance congresses that we attended once a year, since he was the leader of the dance group of the main church.

Suddenly, the church begins to grow, it went from being in the parking lot to having to make modifications to the house so that more people could enter, it seemed that the church would have a rebirth.

At that time there was a restructuring in the praise group and they had "reengaged" me.

In the midst of that, I believed that the pastor really wanted to do things right and I gathered courage. I came up with the great idea of telling him some things that I considered were wrong in the praise group. I did it because of my love for the praise group and because I was part of that first glory and I wanted it to return to those glory times.

Well, I didn't know that they would punish me with something that would change my life forever. I did not know that the man was friends of those who had previously conspired to throw me out of the ministry and planned revenge for saying the bad things that I said were in the praise group.

The pastor told me: "Well, I'm going to put you in charge of the ministry for a few days while the ministry apostle comes for a special 3-day activity. "He's going to have to lead the praise for those three days, you have to choose the songs and rehearse with the musicians and prepare everything."

I almost died with the news because I had never led a service, it always happened that someone else led the service and it was over to me to sing adorations, I would sing what I had to, then I would go to my place in the choir while the praise director He continued to lead the praise.

I didn't know what to do, I gathered my courage and said "Ok, no problems." From what I understand, their idea was that I would not accept or that I would be embarrassed in that special activity and they almost succeeded. In the group were still my uncles and the other two people who were part of the previous conspiracy to remove me from the praise group, so you can imagine what awaited me. Well, I didn't imagine it.

I met with the entire group, including them, and asked them to suggest dates for rehearsals, at which point there was a month left for the activity. Everyone gave their opinion, including them, and together we established a rehearsal schedule. My uncles approached me and told me to count on them to support me because they had more experience than me, but nothing could be further from the truth.

After we all established the rehearsal schedule and after my uncles had told me that they were going to support me, since they had experience in directing praise, neither they nor any of those who had previously conspired to remove me from the praise group attended. even to one of the trials.

The oldest of my sisters, who at that time was also part of the praise group, told me "No, my son, I'm not going to be sad with you." How nice the family is, right?!

Only two people supported me, my younger brother who played the drums and a friend of his who played the guitar, between the three of us we kept going and despite all the adversities I decided to continue.

I had never led a rehearsal before, I had never led a service before and I had a special activity with the apostle of the ministry and almost everyone abandoned me, even my own family who I had in the praise group who had corroborated for the second time that in They were actually my enemies.

The day came and they wanted to be in the praise and of course I let them. The truth is, the first day was a disaster. My nerves and lack of experience betrayed me. Besides, I've always had problems with my nerves and I'm not on medication, by the way.

I came home all unmotivated, I was just crying, maybe everyone was still waiting for the nice movie story that everything turned out well for the one they underestimated, well no, the first day was horrible and after crying and licking my wounds I said to myself "I already did it." "All the ridicule I could make, all the embarrassment I could make has passed, I can't make a fool of myself any more than I already did, so relax and go ahead."

Already on the second day, with the mentality that I couldn't make myself more ridiculous than I had done, I had more courage and rehearsed with my two faithful ones, my brother and his friend. Of course, the rest did not appear at the rehearsal, but they did appear at the night service and obviously I left them and as I felt freer and less nervous because I knew that I could no longer make a fool of myself and be more embarrassed than the day. above, miraculously everything turned out better.

On the third day everything went well and I left changed. What I learned from that experience transformed me! Not only because I could already lead a service, but it created a mentality in me that if God makes me understand that what I am doing is the right thing, even if no one supports me I will continue.

The other lesson I learned concerns family. That day my brother and his friend showed me that they were family and my uncles and my sister showed me that they were not family, I do not hold a grudge against them, but they are things that must be made clear soon. Jesus said Who are my mother and my brothers? (Matthew 12:48,49)

And I began to learn about dealing with emotions and betrayals and after a failure to shake it off and move on.

I would like that one day that young man and my younger brother read this writing and know that I am still grateful to them.

After this they began to have me lead worship from time to time, I still did not feel comfortable leading praise, I was still that shy child with the limitations that a person with Asperger's has, but with the potential that the Holy Spirit gives.

CHAPTER 6
Time to Leave.

The church began to grow again in quantity, but it became poorer in true Christianity. The pastor was a Trojan horse who had Judaism inside him, but very liberal.

At the same time that we celebrated the Sabbath, which by the way at the beginning we didn't even know what they were doing with us, we celebrated Holy Communion in the most despotic way we had ever seen.

The pastor insisted that the holy supper that we used to participate in was very religious, that we had to prepare ourselves, that it was a dinner and that at a dinner you eat everything, that at that time it was bread and wine, because it was what the culture I dined in that region at that time and it is a celebration that should be joyful.

Therefore the celebration of the Holy Supper became anything but holy. An immense disorder such as occurred in the church of Corinth and that the Apostle Paul wanted to correct.

And the disorder in the Holy Supper was only a reflection of the general disorder in the church, where the world had become so mixed with the church that there was no longer any difference between the one and the other.

There were no messages about sin and repentance, only complacent messages. Looking at it carefully, the pastor was unfortunately ahead of his time because today those types of pastors proliferate and fill churches and the largest churches are of that type.

Meanwhile, God had been warning my parents for months that it was time to leave there, but there were many excuses:

-If we leave there, where do we go?

-We have been here for years and the boys grew up in this church.

-Here we already have leadership.

And so a thousand excuses.

Unfortunately, we didn't want to get out the right way and then God had to choose the strong side of him.

Everything happened in the following way:

The pastor asked my dad to preach on a Sunday, but he didn't think about preaching about sin or anything like that, but my dad was already fed up and couldn't help it and when in the middle of the sermon my dad started talking about sin. The pastor stood up from his place and angrily took away the microphone and began a small argument that ended with the entire family getting up from our seats and leaving the church.

Our friends from church hugged us and cried with us as we left the church...

Expressing what we felt at that moment is quite difficult, because it was a combination of many things, knowing what is happening and at the same time not knowing what was really happening. Hundreds of memories passing through our heads while a part remembered all the times my parents talked about how God let them know that we should get out of there.

We got home, I don't know if there was a conversation, I only remember silence. From there, I think my sister never congregated again, my younger brother never took the gospel seriously again and really in the future no one helped him do so.

CHAPTER 7
A new beginning.

After the resounding departure of the previous congregation, we were all lost at home. A few months later my parents began to have a time of prayer in the afternoons in the living room of the house. I joined them months later. My father always reproached me for not joining them right away.

The truth is that it took me years to get over that breakup, although at the time of that breakup I was around 17 years old. I think everyone has different assimilation times. I guess they expected that since I had a supposed spiritual maturity, I should quickly assimilate the situation.

Well, people began to join those prayer times. Some time ago I had lost my job and I asked my father to give me one of the rooms on the ground floor of the house that was not used to accommodate him, since we lived on the second floor and to teach English while I found work.

Miraculously, my father agreed, later I will explain why I describe it as a miracle. It began to go very well for me, so much so that I was able to make money to put a floor and plaster the walls, but while I was doing well, the prayer group that met to pray in the living room of the house was also growing and my father found himself in the need to use the place where I taught and they began to meet there.

It is very interesting that when the church was established, walls were knocked down, ceramics were placed, but the ceramics were not enough for the rectangle of my classroom where everything began, you can see that in the added material that I add in this second edition. But let's not get ahead of the story, we are going to continue telling it step by step and although perhaps everyone already wants to read about the skeletons, it is important to know all this history before presenting all the skeletons.

The truth is that my father did not want to be a pastor, they were always afraid of that because they knew the cost and had seen the behavior of other pastors, so as the group continued to grow my father began to look for a ministry that would send a pastor.

In the group there was a woman who always told us about the apostle of the ministry of the church where she congregated in her hometown.

The insistence was so great that my parents decided to listen to this man's sermons. This woman also lent us a case with an entire workshop on Praise and Worship on cassette taught by this man. The workshop was based on the Tribe of Judah. While I was in the praise group, I had attended many Praise conferences, however, that material was of a higher level.

My parents liked his doctrine, I liked, apart from his doctrine, his position regarding biblical praise, because there are very few pastors who are worshipers or understand what praise really is, he until today is understood in that area.

One day they informed my father that this apostle was going to come to our country and my father decided to go talk to him so that he could send a pastor. My father, for some reason that I do not understand, since he never liked me, among the people who were going to accompany him, he decided to take me and the trip was quite an event for us because of how God spoke to my father since we arrived at the city one day before the service.

The preaching shocked us and I was shocked that unlike all the men of God I had met, even the pastors of that same ministry, this man was approachable, he did not have a security circle or entourage that prevented people from speaking. with the. At the end of the sermon, he greeted everyone, I was close, but I felt sorry for him and I only stayed about two meters away from him.

Then my father met with him and the answer surprised my dad. THE message was "You came to find a shepherd for those people, but you are the shepherd of those people"

CHAPTER 8

Beginning of the pastoral ministry of my parents and first skeletons.

After returning from the trip with the surprise in tow, my parents had to face the reality of the pastorate. Practically, we continued as we were, but no longer waiting for someone to take charge but with my parents carrying the responsibility of the pastorate and once again with the firm decision not to make the same mistakes that they had seen in all the churches where they were. had gone through, much less done the same abuses of power they had seen.

Time would show them that more than a confession was enough, because power, if not handled with humility, ends up bringing out the worst in human beings and a pastorate makes many believe that they have the power. But let's not get ahead of ourselves, let's continue with the beginning of this new stage.

As I mentioned in the previous chapter, we continued to grow and we had to break down walls to expand the congregation, to the point that we still had to use the workshop land. At that point the alarms went off, because the workshop provided security of provision and when my father gathered us together to tell us that they were going to make the decision to remove the workshop to expand the church, there was concern among everyone.

Our father added that probably our lifestyle to which we were accustomed would also change because we would probably no longer have as large an income of money as we had with the workshop, since we would depend on people's tithes and offerings.

In the end we accepted the decision with concern, but in case it had a certain amount of emotion because it seemed interesting to me to see how my parents would function as pastors after repeating for years that if they had to be pastors they would not make the same mistakes and abuses that they saw others commit.

CHAPTER 9

God Explodes the Balloon by Alias Martin García.

The church grew and so did I, I remember that when we started in what was my small English classroom my mother led the worship and I had not yet gotten the big church chip and my mother one day asked me to sing some songs and my answer was: How, if I haven't rehearsed? To which she replied, "You should always be prepared." There my big church chip came out and I understood everything, needless to say, that serves me well to this day.

Sometime later I had one of the greatest learnings I could have, because as time went by I became a "Safe Shot". No matter how cold and apathetic a place was, if you wanted the presence of God to manifest in the place, go to Alias Martin García to worship and that's it. What he did was take the microphone and already, the presence of God was manifested in the place. Then I had a wonderful experience of freedom where in the middle of worship the holy spirit led me to sing praises with power and now that shy person who could only sing worships turned out to now also sing praises, he was already an effective and complete worshiper.

Butooo, but being a safe shot began to make me become arrogant, I already knew that no one moved it like me and I became too inflated and at one point the safe shot was no longer a safe shot, but for my good God made his presence away from me and the big problem was that I had known her presence since I was a child and I became addicted to her and not having her was my death.

In my years in the church, I had seen many people sing and what mattered to them was that the songs turned out well and for them it was already a success. But I was not like that, I had become addicted to the presence of God and it was not enough for me that everything turned out well musically. It used to happen that I finished leading a worship service and everyone congratulated me, but I would lower my head in shame because I knew that his presence had not been manifested and I would not raise my head until I left the church, I felt too ashamed.

They didn't understand me, when they saw me with a sad face even when everything had gone well for me and even when everyone congratulated me, they were disconcerted.

I cried day and night begging God to give me back what I had, but nothing! I went from loving when I saw my name on the list of those who had to lead the services to praying that it didn't appear.

I spent 6 bitter months in that, when I wanted to throw in the towel the unexpected happened. One Tuesday I saw on the list that I had to direct on Sunday and I said to myself "Here I am going to be embarrassed again." I had my rehearsals with the same sadness as the other months, but God had prepared the restitution, and on Sunday, when I took the microphone, I felt that same electricity, that same atmosphere that when I was in the last row of the choir and his presence made Let him raise his voice and the whole church would be filled with his presence, what he felt when he was a sure shot.

Suddenly I felt the same again, but I wasn't the same. Yes, later I made other mistakes as a worshiper, but haughtiness was never one of them again. I understood that I have nothing, I am nothing, I have no voice, I have no charisma, I have nothing, I have nothing that can make him manifest, I can manipulate him, it is not because he is me, it is because he is him.

It's just his grace and it's quite an honor that he shows me when someone adores him. I met people who manipulate emotions, I met people who only like to put on shows, I couldn't be any of that, and I didn't want to, what I wanted was him. From that moment on I never again began to lead praise as someone who was superfluous, but rather as someone who had nothing and was totally dependent.

Since then, every time I have been asked what it takes to be a worshiper, my answer has always been "A heart that is contrite and humbled, you, O Lord, will not despise" Psalm 51:17

Once a young man asked me what it took to be a worshiper and when I responded with that verse he was not satisfied because he was expecting a longer conversation where I would tell him a thousand things, but the truth is that that verse says it all. . I paid a very high price to discover it, but it was necessary.

CHAPTER 10
We continue Palante.

Throughout this process, my father was still being recognized as a man of God. Previously he was recognized in the city for his talents as an evangelist and for how God used him to deliver the demon-possessed. I always remember stories that there were demonized people in his room and my father still had half a block to go to where the demonized person was and the person shouted "No, not him!"

Today I think that this was even a strategy of the devil to boost my father's ego, which would later cause great harm to him and the entire family.

Well, my father was no longer recognized only in the city, but he was already invited to preach in the churches of the ministry to which we belonged, he was loved by many and idolized by the people in the church, obviously being idolized was nothing. well, and along with preachings of honor to the man of God, of loyalty and that if they said anything about the man of God or contradicted him, a thousand curses would befall him, almost absolute obedience was assured.

While all this was taking its toll on the family, and of everyone in the family, the one who suffered the most from my father's arrogance was me. My father was the pastor, he had power over everyone, including me who was not the most beloved of him. His contempt for me was so great that one day I had to ask my uncles to tell me the truth and tell me that, if I was really his son, they seriously confirmed it.

On another occasion I found myself having to ask my mother if my father hated me. I told her to be honest, that I was already prepared for the truth. Besides, he had already done too many things to me for me to be clear, but I needed to hear it. her. Her response was that yes, my father had a certain "thing" for me.

Obviously, I told myself that I was giving him reasons to do so, since I remembered that my other two brothers left school to work in the workshop and when I told him that my desire was to study for him, it was a disappointment apart from that I did not share cultural issues of the family as it was to swear.

Yes, even if you don't believe it, in my family, being pastors, it was common to use rudeness and when scolding us, calling us "Piece of Shit" and I didn't like that way of speaking, much less being Christians, and my father saw that as believing me more. that they. But since I was a child I have believed that Christians should be different even in the way we speak.

I considered all of this to give him reasons to hate me. For her part, my mother was always my defense until a certain point.

My father used his power as a pastor to discipline me whenever he wanted for whatever reason he wanted. I always remember one time when one of my sisters ate something from a small warehouse we had and he told me "I'm sure it was you, if you don't accept that it was you, I'll put you in discipline."

For those who don't know how to "put someone in discipline" means that he can no longer do anything in the church, in my case it meant that he could no longer lead worship or do anything.

At that moment I responded that he could not answer that I had been when the truth is that I had not been, his response was "You are in discipline" and he put me in discipline for six months.

On another occasion, my sister and I were rehearsing with the church dance group and I told a young woman that she should dance with more passion. This girl mentioned it to the pastor and once again he disciplined me.

The truth is he used his power as a pastor to vent all the rage he had on me. Everything anyone told him about me he took as true and he disciplined me.

In my parents' process as pastors, I suffered more injustices than can be counted. And while all that was happening, he continued to be loved and idolized by the people of the church and all the churches in all the cities where they invited him.

Apart from that, miracles occurred through him in such a way that it was impressive. I remember that several times it happened that he did horrible things to me on Sundays before the services began and then after the sermon he asked people to come by to pray for them for healing and while he was praying and the people were shouting saying that they had been healed, he would stare at me. fixedly. I think that was one of the most diabolical things I saw a minister do at that time, later he himself would do worse things to me.

Obviously, there was no one to talk to, what there was a thousand questions towards God without answers.

One of the worst and most horrible moments I can remember occurred with my oldest sister. This sister of mine had always enjoyed preference because she had been prayed to God for years and when God gave her she enjoyed his predilection in all areas.

This sister, without needing to work, since we were well off financially, asked my parents to let her work and my parents finally agreed, but when my sister left work she went to a club that was close to where she worked and she used to tell her my parents that her bosses were bad, that every week they made her work overtime when in reality my sister was in the club.

I mentioned it to my mother, but telling her that was talking to them, criticizing their idol, and like anyone who criticizes their idol, the conversation didn't go well and we argued, but it wasn't an out-of-this-world discussion.

My father was not at home at that time when he arrived, my mother told him the situation and to my surprise, my father, the pastor, at 12 at night, kicked me out on the street for arguing and talking about his idol. I remember the words were "Bearing False Testimony."

My mother kept telling him not to throw me out of the house, but in the end she let him do it.

I was outside the house at 12 at night with my clothes in two black bags and not knowing where to go. In the end I ended up going to the family home of the official boyfriend of the oldest of my sisters, if she was the one with the problem.

While there I lost my job, so since I lost my job, I decided not to eat, because I couldn't afford food. Throughout all of this my mother asked about me from time to time, but that was it.

At one point I had not eaten for so many days that I went to my maternal grandparents' house to ask them to let me stay there and they agreed for me to stay for a while. I still couldn't get a job and my father demanded that if he wanted to return, he had to go ask for forgiveness. I kept saying to myself: "I'm sorry, why did I not do anything wrong?"

Meanwhile, several times I met brothers and leaders in the church on the street and they crossed on the other sidewalk, others from the church that I considered friends saw me and turned away. That destroyed me inside.

Some time later they themselves would tell me that my father told them that if they saw me not to talk to me because I was demon-possessed and that just by talking to me the demons could hit them. It is clear that the reality is that he did not want them to talk to me and for me to tell them my version and for them to believe me. My head kept wrestling with the idea of why God was allowing so much injustice.

In the end my grandmother told me that she should go and ask my father for forgiveness because they couldn't have me there anymore. I don't think I ever expected that my grandmother, my own grandmother, could do that to me, but previous situations had shown that the strong part of my family was not loving me.

In the midst of all that, I did not understand how a just God was allowing all that and in the end, I had to do it, I went home and asked my parents for forgiveness, but my father wanted to humiliate me even more and told me that I should ask for forgiveness. to him before the whole church and to the whole church. I responded that I had to give myself time because that was not easy for me.

The first day I attended a service after that was horrible. All the accusatory looks at me and the comments I had to hear were horrible and things didn't get better until months later. I can't forget one time we were in a service and the pastor asked everyone to pray for the brother next to them, well the one who was next to me the only thing he needed was to say "Lord have mercy on this mangy dog." that I have next to me." Without a doubt they were horrible moments, just going to the service to encounter the stares, the pointing fingers, the bad faces and the comments, was already an immense act of bravery.

One Sunday morning I told my father that I already felt courage to ask for forgiveness in front of the entire church. He responded to me with one of the most diabolical faces that I can remember "This is not when you want, now you are going to do it when I feel like it." He told me that just before going up to the altar to preach.

What followed was quite predictable, my mind could not understand how God could allow so much injustice, apart from the fact that I did not understand how he could continue using him to heal the sick and how people continued to idolize him and I began to try to commit suicide, during that time I had three attempts. of suicide, but in each one I had miraculous salvation, supernatural things happened like one time I had a blade and just when I was going to pass it through my veins the blade came off my hand and flew and disappeared and no matter how hard I looked for it, I couldn't I found her.

On another occasion, with a newly purchased Schick blade that came in a red packaging, I took it out of the packaging and ran it through my veins and it didn't cut and I kept repeating to myself "But I just bought it."

Already after the third time I saw surprising things happen I said to myself "God doesn't want me to do this, so I'm going to have to find a way to deal with this" unfortunately in searching for "those ways" I made many mistakes, but I also found refuge in laughter and I began to remember an experience that I had had many before when my life was honestly no better and returning from high school head down I heard a voice that told me "smile for me" and I quickly raised my head and looked everywhere and there was no There was no one and at that moment I understood that it was God and I raised my head and tried to be happy. But everything that I experienced afterwards had made me forget that experience and after those three failed suicide attempts and remembering the experience I had with God when I was studying in high school, I tried to drain it there.

As for the family situation, after a few months everything blew up in my parents' faces and their idol collapsed because everything became known, my sister's adventures became known to everyone. Like a fool I waited for my parents to apologize to me or at least vindicate me in front of people, but it never happened. That was the first of many times they showed me that they are not the type to admit their mistakes or ask for forgiveness.

Life continued and I continued to become the worst enemy not only of my father but also of my mother. Why? Well, because if I saw something that I considered was not right biblically, I would tell her. I used to do it in her room, lying on the bed, but I would tell her.

Doesn't this bring back any memories of the first chapters that I told you were necessary? Well yes, I became what they were when they started in the gospel and they became those evil pastors who did not like to be told when something was not biblical and they would expel them from the church or place them in discipline. In the end they did do the same thing that they said they were not going to do. But even knowing that they would hate me, I told them things.

Like one time, one of the praise directors was unfaithful to her husband and it was known to everyone and my mother, who was in charge of the praise group, kept letting her lead the services because there was no other person in the praise group to lead the services. as well as she did it, plus, as my mother told me to my face when I confronted her with it, "I haven't seen her doing it so I'm not going to do anything."

And so, everything he saw told him. And what pastor likes that? Well, no bad pastor likes that, pastors love it when everyone applauds what they do and I wasn't like that.

CHAPTER 11
Woman "X" Appears on Scene.

My father continued to discipline me for anything, but this time the surprise would come from my mother. My mother, with everything and everything, had always been my defense in front of my father, but my mother had a detail that the devil knew, my mother never had friends, she always had a lack of love because she did not have a father and her mother always had preferences for others. of his daughters and my father was not a lover as I mentioned in the first chapters.

So my mother had a great lack of affection and then a woman appears, actually the first woman who came to create separation between my mother and me, well, the truth is my mother had problems with us, her children because of her. .

This woman has been in the congregation almost since we began meeting in the living room to pray, but she had never interfered in the family or anything. Since she was almost from the beginning, my parents placed her as secretary of the church and then, without having any spiritual gift or ability, they placed her as a leader, then a deacon and today I believe she is an elder.

And I say what I say regarding this "woman middle of the service because I didn't know how to lead a prayer service.

This woman began to offer my mother affection and she appreciated it and as we say around here she "Bought Her" to the point that my mother blindly believed everything. With my mother's approval, this woman interfered in the family that even dared to order us around. She would come home and say, "Why hasn't she washed?" You start sweeping!

I remember a situation where this woman did something to me and she came first and told my mother. When I got home, I didn't say anything to my mother and I just waited. When my mother came out to scold me, I told her "I'm not going to tell her." nothing even to defend myself because you must know how I am, you formed me, if you want, ask the Holy Spirit" my mother's response was surprising and disappointing; Her response was "I don't need to ask the Holy Spirit anything because woman "X" already told me everything."

I ended up losing respect for my mother's spirituality because of things like that and as I said, it was only the first one because another one would come and displace the first one, but not completely, but this new one would make her make worse mistakes. But we go for a while with my father and the family in general.

Meanwhile my father remained the same and dared to preach three or four times a year about love and in each sermon about love while he preached to each of the children, we left the church because we couldn't stand so much hypocrisy, but the People in the church either didn't realize that or they just didn't want to notice. I still don't understand if they were very stupid, very well manipulated or all three at the same time.

As the church grew and grew, we had churches in two nearby cities and all growing. While my dad was becoming very skilled at manipulation, deception and hypocrisy. In the first edition I did not tell this, but it does provoke me to tell it in this 2nd edition.

Well, the truth is that we were in the service, there was a sister leading the praise and everything was looking very ugly, when the sister finished, he came forward and said, "If anyone here did not feel the presence of God while this sister was singing, it is because He is dead, because this was wonderful" and obviously the little sister who led the praise felt great.

But at home we had a custom that after the service ended and we got home while we were having lunch, we would share about how the service had been, and that day after my father had praised that girl for her skeading the praises when we got home, What he did was criticize her, he said "How horrible how that woman led the praise, I don't know how people put up with her, besides that was dead."

While I didn't understand how the thing worked, a while ago I had praised it in public and now, I was destroying it? Then I understood, praising her in public ensured that the woman loved him and the first tool used to manipulate someone is to flatter them.

For my part, I made several mistakes because my emotional life was chaos, I didn't understand anything, I knew that suicide was no way out, but I couldn't find a way out, the one I considered the love of my life had died, I started dating a girl of the church, but she was an idolater of my father, after a few years I ended up still loving her, but living what I lived at home I couldn't be with someone who was an idolater of my father.

I kept rambling, I practically harassed one girl, I had problems with another. I needed to feel appreciated because I felt that God allowing so much injustice was an enemy rather than a friend. I think if someone had offered me drugs I would have tried them. I've been asking for forgiveness from people I hurt for about 5 years and I'm not done yet.

CHAPTER 12
The Other Arrives, The "Y" Woman

If The First One Brought Problems To our Home, This One Would Bring Problems Even To The Church.

After a long time of my mother's blindness with the woman "X" and after having problems with all the children and with many people from the church, the woman "X" took advantage of the fact that my mother believed her everything to do a little disaster in the church, my mother finally lost her blindness with that woman "X". Well, just a little.

But behind the scenes was a woman who had arrived at the church a few months ago and had two musical sons between 18 and 20 years old. This woman "Y" little by little won my mother's heart with details, until she won it completely and that meant that not only would she have preference, but that her children would also have preference and not only preference with my mother but with the whole church.

But these boys did not depend entirely on their mother to win over people, they themselves had certain skills and soon became loved by the entire church and even by my father. There are people who have a charisma, a way of speaking, of making themselves loved, and they had that.

I always remember a conversation that the eldest of the two sons of woman "Y" had with my father at home where he told my father that he had never seen a pastor like him and that he would obey him in everything and that he would not do anything without communicate them. My father entered the room where the rest of us were with his chest puffed out, saying that those were God's boys.

I don't know if I mentioned it before, but like any arrogant and proud person, my father loved flattery and if you flattered him enough you could have him eating out of your hand and these young men quickly detected this and used it to their advantage.

I'm going to tell something that I didn't tell in the first edition, but I'm going to do it now that I feel more freedom to write. You know, as I realized that my father liked flattery and I felt the need to be loved by my father, for a while, well for a few days, I began to treat him with flattery as he liked and for the first time Once in my life I felt loved by him. He began to treat me well until I gave me a place in the church.

But I was having a big problem inside me, and the problem was that I felt DIRTY and hypocritical and then an internal struggle began because I wanted to be loved by my father and by flattering him I had achieved it, but at the same time I couldn't stand the feeling of feel dirty In the end I went away one night to make a decision, and with a lot of pain and tears I decided to stop treating him the way he liked even knowing that my life would once again be a miserable life because I would have to go back to the contempt, mistreatment and humiliations that he was used to subjecting me to, but I made that decision because I could no longer stand feeling dirty. And just as I imagined it happened.

Returning to the topic of the children of the woman "Y" Soon these boys were already playing in the praise group, without even being very faithful to anything or anything and without even showing a grain of spirituality.

Boys who spoke very nicely put the entire church in their pockets and practically everyone loved them, for a while I was friends with them, but there was one thing that the eldest of the two told me that didn't agree with me one bit and he made that I should separate myself from the group that with them; This young man told me that he did not need to pray much to lead services in the church, that all it took was saying the right words at the right time and you could make people cry.

With that phrase they revealed to me who they really were and they soon showed me that it was true because, with the preference that my two parents had for them, it didn't take long for them to lead the Sunday services and yes, just as they told me, just like that The older of the two brothers did it and it worked. The guy didn't need spirituality, with manipulation of emotions and with a church without spiritual discernment he could make people cry. -Any resemblance to modern Christian groups is not purely coincidental-

At that moment, it was a surprise to me how this boy had such ability to manipulate people's emotions. Nowadays it is normal for it to happen, but at that time not so much.

I couldn't find anyone to talk to about this, I spoke what I thought about these boys with my girlfriend, yes the one who was an idolater of my father and she confessed to me that this boy, even knowing that she was my girlfriend, was courting her, but since she was an idolater of my father, if my father said that they were from God she had to repeat it. I talked about it with a friend from the praise group and it seems that she told it to other people and after a few days all the people were making fun of me because they said that I was envious of them because they had more of God than me.

However, I treated them well because they loved these "beauties" and once I was singing with them, while I was singing, I prayed to God and told him that I wanted to be like them, that everyone loved them and no one loved me. loved. While I was doing that I heard a voice that audibly told me "I didn't call you for that."

You reader can believe it or not, but I am telling the truth of what happened, just as it happened to me. I know that there are people who don't believe that God speaks like that, but that's how it happened to me and I'm not going to stop saying it because there are people who don't believe in these things.

After that I continued with my thing, my mother was going to have a musician play who had not even been a convert for two months and I told her that I didn't think it was the right thing to do, but she put it on anyway. Who was going to contradict the decision? of "the woman of God"? but I considered it my duty to say things, even when they didn't pay attention to me.

Today I have a biblical basis that gives me security that I was doing the right thing, because if I didn't say it, I was an accomplice and I have always said that it is enough for me to deal with my own sins and then I also have to face the consequences for being an accomplice to the sins. of others.

Then it happened that one Sunday it was my turn to lead the praise, and after I finished, I was very sweaty and I had the habit of looking for a cloth to wipe off the sweat and I remembered that there was a cloth that I liked in a little room that almost no one entered and There I went to look for my cloth and what I found was not exactly my cloth but the two youth leaders having sexual relations while the pastor was preaching. I went into shock and lost my speech for two hours.

After I came out of the shock I told my mother, and at the youth service of the week she let the girl lead the worship, I told her that I did not agree and she replied that there was no one who led the service as well as she.

Meanwhile, the idolatry with the boys continued, at that time I was not a worship leader, but I was in charge of being in charge of the rehearsals at my mother's command. My father held a church meeting where he put my mother's friend's eldest son as the praise leader while repeating something like: "this one is going to make the praise group count, not like the other one" that is me. .

Everything started "well", I was relegated. These kids had my parents so in control that even the rules that my parents established they broke and my parents preferred to eliminate the rules that they themselves established rather than tell them anything.

My mother had a rule that no worshiper who did not attend the weekly services could lead on Sundays, by the way, they made the rule for me, I worked until 8 at night and I could not be in almost any church service. week, so they made sure that he could not lead any worship. But it turns out that these kids, even though one of them was the worship leader, didn't like going to the weekly services because he was "working" and they did let him lead on Sundays, but not me, in the end they ended up eliminating Rule.

Before continuing with the other rules that my parents eliminated because of these kids, I just realized that above I wrote working in quotes and I remembered something very funny that happened, it turns out that it was a rehearsal day and one of the kids, The worship leader himself called my mother and told her that he couldn't attend because he was working. After a while, a cousin's wife came home and asked my mother, "And the worship leader didn't come to the rehearsal?" And my mother responds "No, he's working" And my cousin's wife responds "uhmmm, I was at the mall a moment ago and he was going into the movie theater with his girlfriend, but if he said he was working, "I was working then."

My mother had a rule that all worshipers had to receive discipleship. They told my mother that they were not there to receive discipleship but to dictate it. And what did my mother do? Well, what the babies said about her, she made them disciple.

On another occasion something quite sad and comical happened. My parents put the youngest of the "Y" woman's children in charge of the church radio even though I had asked them to put me because my younger sister had asked me to quit my job because she considered that I was They were exploding, which the truth was a lie, but that's another story. The truth is that my mother preferred to place her friend's son rather than me.

After this boy was placed in charge of the radio, it happens that suddenly the radio inputs begin to decrease. My father did not charge anyone a fee, but everyone who had a program on the radio only gave an offering, so practically everyone who wanted to have a program on the radio was given the opportunity.

But at the same time, it meant that the entries were not many, but even so this did not explain the drop in economic income from the radio so my father set a trap for the boy and he fell flat! The boy was stealing! The only joy this gave me is that it meant that my father was no longer so blind, but my mother, well keep reading uhmmm, you better keep reading.

I know no one is a fortune teller, but could you guess my mother's attitude? Do you know what she said? Her response was "It wasn't his fault, it's just a spirit of the devil attacking him."

Before that, something very interesting had already happened. As, according to me, I had a good relationship with the boy who was in charge of the radio, without my father knowing I entered the radio and saw some strange things and I told the young man "Be careful with that, because people may think "that you are stealing money from the radio"

I think I did that on a Saturday, to my surprise on Sunday after the service my mother called me to a meeting and when I saw the boy and the boy's mother there, immediately my mother started talking and said "This meeting is because you called." to this thief boy" I was astonished, the surprise was immense because first I considered that despite everything I had a friendship with that boy, even though I knew that they were not true worshipers but showmen, I never treated them badly, and he had a special affection for him in particular because he believed that he was not as false as his brother.

After I reacted from the surprise I told the boy "I told you what? What did I call you?" And then I told my mother and his mother how things had happened, but obviously my mother demanded over and over again that I had to apologize to the boy as well as his mother because that was what her friend, the boy's mother, demanded. In my mind she kept repeating to me: Could it be that I explain it to her with apples?

Before continuing, I would like you, who are reading this book, to stop for a moment and think: Do I have friends like that? Does my pastor have friends like that? What blind them and make them commit injustices? Always remember that my idea with this book is not to take out clothes in the sun, if that were the case I would include my name and the names of each one. What happened to my mother can also happen to you, your pastor, your wife, or your church leaders, including me who is writing this book. That is why it is important to have an emotional life where the devil and/or people cannot take advantage of our emotional needs.

Let's continue

Then, while I was living in the city where I am, I had to spend a few days in my city, that is, at my parents' house and while there they were reorganizing the radio and placing the new manager who would replace the boy who according to my mother was not a thief. , but rather that "a demon was attacking him" in the midst of this restructuring, my father had the perception that some radio equipment had been "Lost", but he had no idea which ones.

At that moment something very interesting happened, because my father always prohibited my access to the radio, but when that happened, I told my father "Please let me check the radio because I know what was there because I donated several of the equipment." My father's face was quite a poem when I told him that.

I had never told him that in my life, only my younger sister's husband and one other person knew. And to me it felt cool that I wouldn't be allowed on the radio. I felt good because he showed myself that I was doing it for God and not for people.

I remember that I didn't have a computer, but I donated one to the radio station and that made me very happy, because I wasn't giving away what I had left over and I did it even though I was prohibited from entering. Those things showed me that it was for love of God and not for acceptance or honor of men.

I think that one of the most heretical things and that showed me that my mother had lost all fear of God, occurred when, as we were about to start a rehearsal, my mother got up, made us stand up, we gathered in a circle and He told us that God had told him that I wanted to steal his praise group.

I was stunned, I looked at her and smiled, I didn't respond or defend myself. At the end of the rehearsal, one of the worship directors approached me and told me "I know that is a lie because I saw and heard when the woman "Y" was telling her that and now she comes and says that God told her." I responded, "Are you going to tell me? I'm the one who knows best that it's a lie."

After all that, the idolatry continued, but with surprise, and the surprise began because the worship leader boy went to a Christian concert and in the middle of the anointing (sarcasm) he fathered a son with a girl from another city, but he continued ministering. and serving as worship director as if nothing had happened, but when the girl saw that she was pregnant, she went to look for him and appeared at the church. I witnessed none of this, when I came home from work I heard about a commotion and I asked the son of woman "X" (see previous chapter) very casually if he was hitting on me and he told me everything.

The truth is that they wanted to pretend as if nothing happened, in the end they paused the boy as worship director, it was surprising that my mother made it very clear that they had not removed him, but that he was temporarily "On Pause." Could it be that you can see the difference between me being disciplined for six months for telling someone to dance with passion and this boy just pausing? And the worst had not happened, because the worship leader boy had a girlfriend, who was officially presented with great fanfare, who was obviously not the same girl with whom the leader boy had fathered the child.

This girl did not know anything about the matter and she found out because at a church activity my mother agreed to present the son "from the concert." The boy's girlfriend was in the church at that special activity and upon seeing her boyfriend who stopped by to introduce her his newborn son with another woman runs crying through the entire church.

Do you want to guess what my mother said? Which, by the way, my ears heard and no one else told me. No, I don't think they will even guess it in a hundred thousand years. My mother said "She is ridiculous, as if she were a saint." And she said that the leader boy's girlfriend was not a saint because before being dating the leader boy she had had other boyfriends. But if we have some humanity and feelings we would understand this girl's actions.

As for me, through my mother, he was being sent along with some leaders to help with Sunday services at one of the churches we had in a nearby town that had few people.

The truth is, for me it was wonderful, apart from the fact that I could no longer stand listening to my father's preaching or his manipulation of people if he boasted of his power to heal. In the church that my father pastored they never made me lead prayer services, something that I always dreamed of and I think that in 20 years I only said a word twice and there in that city in front of 10 people I could do it and that was wonderful, sometimes There were only about 5 of them and still for me it was wonderful.

And guess what happened? Don't you want to guess anymore? Well, They started sending the leader boy with me to be restored. I still don't understand that part well, they removed him as leader, but just a few days later they were sending him with me to lead worship in that other city. He was slow, but not slow, slow in the main church but not completely so he wouldn't feel bad.

CHAPTER 13
The Bells Ring.

Being in all this madness of life and looking for an escape, I met a woman online who was from the leadership of the central church in our country, the apostolic ministry to which we belonged. I was already 38 years old at that time. This woman was highly respected as a leader.

She told me that she spoke to the senior leadership about us and since she did not live in the same city where the church was, the senior leadership thought it would be wonderful because they could put us in charge of a church in the city where she lived.

I went to the city where she lived to meet her in person. Things didn't go well at all. Because I was the son of a pastor and she was the son of the central church leadership, it was crazy for me to stay at her house, so we arranged with another sister for me to stay at her house.

When I arrived in the city, my sister had to be urgently hospitalized and I had to sleep at my girlfriend's house, which I didn't like. In all this I am omitting several things that I might add in a third edition.

But I consider that it was my fault because I should have been more cautious.

I returned to my city, for weeks I didn't write messages to her and she did write to me daily, but I didn't respond because I needed to be sure, because I knew that it wasn't just any decision I had in front of me, but things weren't getting better at home and I I always had a dream of serving God and marrying her gave me an escape and I could also serve God.

God gave me a word about them in Ezekiel 2:3-10. But I really didn't believe it was God who gave me that word because those people seemed too nice for that word to be about them. Sometime later I would regret not having accepted that word as from God and preparing myself better for the music that I would have to dance to.

We made our courtship official to both our parents and the senior leadership of the ministry, she went and met my parents and we set a date for the marriage. Some brothers from the church assured me that when I arrived in that city they would find me a job, so everything was already planned.

That last week in my city I think I prayed more than at any time in my life, I was very afraid.

I quit my job and left. The youngest of my sisters accompanied me, it was something simple, we only got married civilly.

My sister left and I was left there, in a city where she didn't know anyone and where no one knew me and 7 hours away from anything I knew.

We went to the central church to talk to the leadership, they asked us to find a location to set up a "Semi-virtual" church that they would pay for. The idea of this type of church was to gather people in a place and, using a video beam, project to them the worship of the main church that was transmitted over the Internet and we would be in charge of that.

We took on the task of looking for that place, while we went out to evangelize on Saturdays with the group of people, we had here plus an evangelism group that they sent from the central church and on Sundays we met at home and watched the service online while we found the store.

The brothers who assured me that I would have a job just upon arriving in the city ignored me. Shortly after, the severance money they gave me at my old job ran out.

We lived at my mother-in-law's house and the woman became quite demanding about what she wanted to eat, so we had to go into debt so that my mother-in-law could eat what she wanted.

Suddenly we had nothing and no one to borrow from. We began to go hungry, sometimes we ate only once a day, other times for lunch, we asked a neighbor for permission to enter his yard and we ate from the mangoes that were on the floor because we were not allowed to cut down mangoes.

For her part, my mother-in-law did manage to eat, but she made her own food apart from herself and didn't give us anything, and she didn't even give my wife, who was her daughter, any food.

Ministerially things were also getting strange. We could not find a place to set up the semi-virtual church, so the central church could not give us any salary and most of the brothers who met with us were quite poor.

And it got more difficult because the pastor of the main church began to preach very heretical things and people began to ask questions, at first my answers began with "He didn't mean that, what happened is that you misunderstood what he really meant." meant"

Then when some began to get upset because they perceived that I was treating them like idiots, things became more difficult for me, my problem was that I knew that the other part of the group was quite idolatrous and if they said that the pastor whom they idolized had made a mistake They were going to hate me. So I was walking through very dangerous terrain.

At the same time that I was struggling with that within me, a transformation occurred because they had a prayer time in the afternoons that they had stopped and when I arrived they considered that they should resume it, but I divided it for myself. During that time of prayer, a micro-worship was held where a word was presented, there was a micro-time of worship and then there was a time of prayer.

For me that was too much, because my parents had never found it pleasant to have me lead prayer services and only twice in 20 years had they had me give a word. The only practice I had in both things was in the three or four months that lasted when I was sent to that small congregation dependent on the church that my father pastored.

I remember that the pressure was such that one day I called my mother on the phone and, crying freely, I repeated, "Why, why didn't you guys put me on? Now I don't know what to do." I remember that my mother did everything possible to He calmed me down and told me that God was going to help me.

As for Sundays, I continued to have the same struggle, with both groups, there came a time when the heresies were so great that a clear position was required of me and I began to tell them the truth, to tell them when the pastor was preaching a heresy. and to explain to them biblically what the truth was.

Obviously, I began to have problems with the group of idolaters. And then I had more problems with everyone in general because I began to notice that every time they went to pray as a group, they took off their shoes. I asked and they explained to me that before I arrived, when they met to pray, God had given them a word. that they were "bare feet" so every time they went to pray, they took off their shoes.

In the best way I could, I explained to them that I did not doubt that God had spoken to them, but that I was sure that God was not referring to them taking off their shoes every time they went to pray, but that it was something more internal.

The explanation was not very well accepted and some said "As long as he is still there I will not visit that house again." For my wife it was horrendous first because most of them were her family and she is very idolatrous towards her family and there was the other party who It was economic, since we were already starving and from time to time one of them would bring us something to eat and the fewer people there were, the less likely they would bring us something. Our relationship that was never good was now getting worse.

I went from being hated by only one part to being hated by the majority for touching their idol with their bare feet and to make matters worse I was going to make things even worse and I realized that when they prayed, if the children said anything They were taken as if it were God himself speaking. Can you guess why? Exact! For the same reason you are thinking, in the prayer times they had before I arrived,

God had given them a word and told them that God was going to use the children greatly.

To make matters worse, they had a person who was convulsing and while he was convulsing in delirium he said things and they also took those things as if it were God himself speaking. In fact, they had a person whom they called the scribe who was in charge of writing in a specially designed notebook. dedicated everything that both the children and the person who was having a seizure said. It was interesting that while the children were talking in their transverse or the person was talking in his delirium after having a seizure, the person who was in charge of writing everything down repeated over and over again "God keep speaking, your servants can hear."

It was too much for me and I told them: "No, my dears, that's not like that, I don't doubt that God also spoke to you about those children, but everything must be filtered through the Bible and I shouldn't accept anything that 7-year-old children say. in a supposed trance as if it were God himself speaking and even more so when those children don't even pray at home."

Furthermore, I added: "you should always test the spirits and not quickly accept everything as if it is from God."

Dale, others who left because it was a heresy for me to say that they had to test the spirits and submit every word to the Bible. More problems with my wife, more problems with people and nothing was going to get better.

We started to have internet problems and sometimes we couldn't see the sermons and that, although on the one hand it was good for me because I no longer had to try to excuse the inexcusability of the heresies that the pastor preached, but on the other hand, my wife told me He said that I had to give them a word and that was another level for me and for every Sunday I had to have a sermon prepared in case the internet went down. If I called my mom crying because she didn't know how she was going to be able to say a little word from Monday to

Friday, now that she also had to prepare a word for Sundays she made my hair stand on end.

While the pastor of the main church continued preaching heresies and I no longer knew what to do, to make matters worse some scandals broke out with that pastor, he appeared on television denying it, but my wife who had been there since the beginning of that church had quite a few acquaintances in the church. church and from a reliable source we were able to learn that, although the pastor denied everything, it was all true.

In the middle of all this mess, my wife began to wage direct war on me because with everything I did that made her family upset and her being so idolatrous towards her family, I took her to the extreme and she and an aunt of hers who still do not know I had gone, they declared an official and direct war on me.

As for the ministry to which we belonged, in the end what was happening was too horrendous, and the apostle of the ministry worldwide did nothing. As I said a few chapters ago, that apostle was very approachable, so I contacted him through Facebook, I had very nice conversations with him, in fact, several publications that I have placed on Facebook were reviewed by him before being published.

But when it came time to speak, the representative of the ministry in the country told me that he only prayed. It did not seem like a correct answer to me because I considered that as an apostle he should behave like the apostles of the Bible and establish order, but not did.

Sometime later my wife told me that we had to leave the mystery, I responded that I had to pray it first, the truth is I was very afraid because it implied that after days of prayer and fasting in the end we would leave the ministry.

When we communicated our decision to those who remained, the hatred towards me increased because they thought that the decision to leave the ministry, others left and there were only 8 people left, including me and my wife.

The dream that made me sacrifice everything to serve God was beginning to fall. Well, it wasn't much, leaving something very horrible for something even more horrible.

In the midst of that, every once in a while my mother would pay for my trip home and from there she would return with some food.

Several months had passed since the last time I had gone and I began to perceive things in my spirit that I did not like. And I told my wife, "I know that we are in great need, but I pray to God that my mother does not call me to go because the holy spirit does not leave me alone with some things that I must tell you."

Three months had passed and I was still with that anxiety and my younger sister called me telling me to go spend a few days at home, so I started to make all kinds of excuses, but my wife told me "you know that we don't have anything to eat." and every time you go there, they give you bags of food." And I repeated, "but things don't look good, God is making me tell them things that I know they don't want to hear."

What the holy spirit was placing in my heart to tell them was that they should leave the ministry and that they had humbled themselves too much in front of that ministry."

In the end my wife convinced me, it was the most stressful trip in the world because I began to fight with God, I began to tell him that please no, why didn't he send someone else, that if I told them that they would get upset with me and they wouldn't. They were going to give me bags of food as always.

Well, I arrived in my beautiful city, I practically didn't sleep discussing the same things with God. After fighting so much with God to not do it, I had to do the same and in the worst way, because the idea was to tell my parents what God sent me to tell them while the three of us were locked in the room, but no, the morning started tense and For the first time in my life as far as I can remember, I yelled at my father and mother in public, I told my mother to shut up and I told my father "You dropped your pants in front of (Pastor's Name)"

What followed was horrendous, my younger sister demanded that she leave the house and that she watch how I left because she was not going to give me money to leave because she was not going to accept that they yelled at her mother. I imagine she meant "to have someone else yell at her" because she has grown tired of doing it over and over again throughout her life. But let's continue.

I started communicating with several friends on Facebook and nothing, only one lent me a little money, then my wife asked to borrow a little more and finally a brother of sound doctrine that I barely knew lent me what was missing, which by the way for me is A milestone because I have never again seen someone of sound doctrine giving away something, rather someone told me on a Facebook page that whoever said that Facebook page was to collect money was only to discuss sound doctrine. In all the years that I have been studying the reform and people of sound doctrine, the only one who has not behaved like a jerk was that young man.

Let's go back to the story. I collected the money, I returned, but it was no longer just that we had no food, but now we had three debts to pay.

For me the moral of everything is that if I had decided from the beginning to obey God what happened would not have happened.

That was not the first time that God gave me words for my parents, but I gave them many words over the phone and in no case did they obey even when each word was fulfilled exactly as I said it. At a certain point they had to leave the ministry and God worried me to tell them to take some time before joining another ministry and made me understand about one in particular that they should not join. I told it to my mother just as God put it in my heart, the truth is, except for that situation, I never told my father about things that God showed me. Well, I told my mother, I told her to please take some time and not to involve me with "X" ministry and she replied: "Of course not, we leaving one are not going to enter another." -The lady is a liar-

To my surprise, a few days later I was on Facebook and I looked at some photos of the Sunday service that a little brother posted, they even had the ministry logo, they didn't even last a year. So in two years they had left one ministry, entered another and left. You have to understand that many pastors are manipulated by telling them that if they do not join a large ministry, their churches will not prosper and my parents had that problem.

On another occasion we felt a great burden on a person that my father was going to place as a pastor in one of the churches in a nearby city and I called my mother and told her on behalf of God to please tell my father not to place as a pastor to that person. My mother told me that he had practically already decided to put it on, but that he had gone into a few days of fasting.

When talking to my younger sister I was able to understand that since several people did not agree with that man being appointed as a pastor, he had gone on a fast to keep quiet and in the end he was going to appoint him anyway with the excuse that God He showed. He did it as is, at the end of his fast, he said that he had already made up his mind and appointed that man as shepherd.

After a while, the man turned the congregation against my father and stayed with the church.

I want to repeat by saying that I hope the reader can understand that my idea with this book is not to expose my clothes to the sun or to humiliate someone or to get even for everything they did to me, because if that were my desire I would write a thousand more things, like every time. that in the middle of church meetings he would humiliate me and I would end up crying in my room or when I was with the praise group and he would stand in the middle just to humiliate me and God is my witness that I am only writing a quarter of everything I experienced in order that the message I want to give is understood and pastors and leaders can be more spiritual and less emotional and even the church can help its pastors.

Another thing I would like people to learn from this book is that sometimes the flock is very responsible for how arrogant their shepherd can become.

I remember having a lot of problems with my dad because he got upset when I called him dad. Automatically, he responded to me "That's why you are not blessed, when you recognize me as a pastor, as the man of God, your life will change." Obviously I was left with a poker face. He loved being called and sometimes even demanded to be called "The Man of God" "The Angel of the Church" - which no one said he wasn't.

He loved the adulation. In the last sermon that I heard from him in person, he said "To be blessed you must prostrate yourself before the man of God" -Damn!-

And the church, so that he wouldn't get upset, played along, they did plays and made him come out with angel wings. We understand that the pastor should be honored, but we must also understand that everyone has to struggle with their ego and people who are very used by God must be very careful with that.

At a certain point my father believed himself to be all-powerful and untouchable because he did evil and injustice to everyone and he continued to be used by God, so, instead of taking it as God's patience, he saw himself as untouchable and I consider that the church had part of the blame for that.

Another important thing, as Paul Washer once said, "There are churches that God's will is for them to spend their entire lives with 100 people because God knows that if they grow more they can be damaged."

The heart of man is deceitful, as an example I can give you that 99% of the things that my parents said they would not do if God called them to the pastorate, they did and I know that the dream of every pastor is to have a large church because he speaks well of him as a pastor, but sometimes a lot of people, a lot of applause, a lot of "There is no man like you in this city" hurts people.

Evidently, my father, apart from himself not learning to control his ego, was damaged by a church that instead of helping him wanted to go along with him and then, as you read, was already demanding that people prostrate themselves before him if they wanted to. be blessed.

Returning to the story of the church, as for the church in general, the praise group became a disaster, I remember that one of the times I went home, two of my nieces arrived that my mother had raised and with whom I was very close. good relationship, they met with me and told me that the praise group became a small group war and that the leader boy became a disaster and then I see my mother, who knew about this whole situation, only worried about the color of the toga they were wearing to use the people of the praise group choir, it was at that precise moment that I understood that my mother had lost all her spirituality for which I valued her so much.

On another trip I found out that one of the men who was part of the choir had had sexual relations with several little sisters from the church and my father's response to that was "Poor boy, he has been without a woman for years and a man has his needs." "And according to what they told me, he insisted that they leave him in the choir.

Note to my beloved leaders who may read this: "When a pastor advocates that kind of thing, be concerned because it is very likely that he is doing the same thing, and in my father's case he was."

As for me, on one occasion, when I had just arrived in this city, the apostle of the ministry to which we belonged, had a morning meeting on Facebook and began to mention a number of people that I had never heard of before: "Charles Finney, Jonathan Edwards, Charles Spurgeon, John Wesley, Wilkerson, Huss, Luther..." he began to talk about some such "generals" and I wanted to know who they were.

Taking advantage of the fact that I didn't have a job, well I didn't have a job, work was going too far, well taking advantage of the fact that I didn't have a job, I started reading and reading and reading, in one hand a book, in the other hand the Bible, then the war that My wife and her aunt had me, they made me study the Bible even more, Well there is no greater motivation to prepare than the opposition.

Then what I read clashed with all the gospel that I had learned, then I had the urgent need to learn what the gospel was because the pastors of the ministry to which I belonged assured that the true gospel was one thing, then I had books from the men of God from before and it was something else, then I read a book by Paul Washer and it confronted me with everything I thought I knew since I was a child, then I read the 4 gospels over and over again and analyzed Jesus, his character, his teachings, his gospel, then I read over and over again. Once Paul's letters, then I read the entire New Testament over and over again and ended up at a crossroads, "either I stayed with everything I had known since I was a child or I accepted what I was learning directly from the Bible."

At a certain moment I stood before God and told him "I have no problems, come on, teach me from scratch, here I am as if I didn't know anything about the Bible, as if I were a recent convert, I am emptying myself of the thousand sermons, of what I believed it was the gospel, which was more based on man's preaching and I decided to obey your word. I felt free, I also felt vulnerable because the truth is that a lifetime in the gospel gives a certain security, but I knew that what I had decided it was the right thing to do.

At that moment I also realized that I had never been a true Christian. I wrote to my friends on Facebook asking for forgiveness for not having given them an example of a true Christian and I started with my new birth.

I wanted to share my joy with my mother, but she ignored me like a dog. A few months after I arrived in this city, I was left without a phone and I remember how excited I was. I asked to borrow a phone to share with my mother everything I was learning and they lent me one of those phones from before that they call "gallito" and I was writing to my mother letter by letter URL ADDRESSES of videos of Wilkerson,

Ravenhill and a moment of other people apart from URL addresses to read the books and various teachings on prayer by Charles Spurgeon so that you understand how horribly difficult and tiring it is I recommend Let them try.

About two months later I had to go to my family and I arrived all excited asking him about each video and each book and I realized that not only had he ignored me, but that he didn't mind admitting that he was interested in what he found interesting. I sent with so much emotion and suffering.

Some time later I realized that at a certain moment she fell into an evil that every Christian can fall into and especially if they have been in the gospel for years and especially if they are or have been a pastor. The problem of "I already know everything that "I should know and no one can teach me anything." And if someone wants to teach them something they make their face as if they were smelling a horrible fart and act with such sobriety!

As for my mother, one time it was something like, "You want to teach me about prayer when I taught you how to pray?"

Several times later I kept trying, but nothing! and the last time I went home 6 months ago, I could see the consequences of this evil that can happen to all of us "It was December, several brothers and some nieces met for dinner and she said a prayer and hearing it was a blessing for me. One of the saddest things, I had not heard her pray for about 2 years and that day I perceived her prayer as if it were old bread. My mother, the person who had taught me to pray, the one who had instilled in me the search for God, had become "Stagnant Water"

Unfortunately, it was not the only sadness for me, because the next day was the Sunday service, I noticed with pain that the praise group had been deserted, that group for which I fought so much, for which I cried so much, but that the final My parents preferred to leave it in charge of my mother's friend's children, who left it in ruins and left, and there was a worship director who looked like a news narrator accompanied by a girl I only recognized as an Instagram model. , and by this I mean the fact that he spent almost every day posting photos of himself on said social network.

While the praise was going on, one of the leaders, woman "X", shouted from behind to try to liven things up. And only memories of the good times came to my mind, and while I cried, photographs that I have on my computer of the times in which the glory of God moved me in the midst of praise and I repeated to myself " If they had listened, if only they had listened"

And the following text came to mind that I once wrote on Facebook about the praise group that I loved so much a few years ago, when I already saw the damage they were doing to my beloved praise group, these young people that my mother idolized:

"MY VINEYARD: I had a vineyard, rather it was not mine, but I loved it like no one else loved it and perhaps like no one else will ever love it, I took care of it from its foundation, I fought to keep it healthy and strong, day and night I spent my strength to make it strong, healthy and beautiful, I tried to scare away the dogs that only wanted its leaves and fruits.

Even when the vineyard keepers beat me and dragged me out of the vineyard, I continued to love it without reservation. The caretakers put other people with knowledge of vineyards in charge of the vineyard, but without love and from afar I tried to take care of it until one day the caretakers completely excluded me, in the end I had to go far away.

The caretakers forgot that beauty is not given to a vineyard by the knowledge one has about vineyards but by the love one has for the vineyard. Today I hear that my vineyard is sick, there are no strong roots in its plants, the leaves are falling, the dogs have shaken my beloved vineyard, there is no longer light in the vineyard that I loved and my heart is spilling out, the vineyard that I loved is no longer It has light, those who were put in charge have made my vineyard something of horror, there is no longer dew from heaven in my vineyard and the whisper of the sky cannot be heard in the middle of it, only rubble remains of how beautiful it once was.

What will become of my beloved vineyard, the one I loved with all my soul? I can only pray to the God of heaven to have mercy on my vineyard, the vineyard that I love with all my soul...Saturday, July 11, 2015 at 13:28 UTC-04:30"

After the "praise" where the news narrator, I mean, the praise director only needed to give the weather forecast, came the preaching. My mother preached, because my father supposedly resigned from the pastorate after several scandals that I do not want to detail, but that I have referred to previously.

A sermon, like you, a pastor or leader reading this, should never preach in your life, a sermon like she once said she would never preach, a sermon where she spent the hour and a half of the sermon throwing "hate" and added 8 or ten spiritual phrases.

My plea, when it is almost time to finish these memories, is that you pastor, you leader, take for yourself and in the flock of God the necessary corrections so that the same thing does not happen in your life as a pastor and in your congregation and not think that this can't happen to you because the truth is it can happen to anyone. My parents are no worse than you, what happened to my mother did not happen to her because she was less wise than you, the truth is that at one point she was very wise and at one point she trusted her own wisdom.

Don't think that what happened to my parents was due to a lack of spirituality, my parents were very spiritual and relied on that. In fact, to this day I don't know a church that prays as much and fasts as much as in my parents' church, however, they are very muddy and my mother is a pit of stagnant water.

One of the problems was that they became confident in how much they prayed, but they did not die. I have never in my life seen my parents ask someone for forgiveness, several months ago I confronted her and she said "I asked God for forgiveness." They have unbroken hearts and have never wanted to be broken and all this can happen to you too, dear Pastor, dear leader. I continue to pray for my parents that God would break their hearts and I dream of seeing the church restored. Maybe at that time I will write another book about how God can restore when people are truly broken and they don't just cry and then continue with the same life.

Regarding my life and "ministry", after meeting 5 people, a great teaching came to me. With everything I had been learning, I wanted those 5 to not be the kind of bad Christians that I was, and I wanted to train them as real Christians, but I ended up learning that you can't make someone into something they want to be.

I understood that they wanted to be new Christians, but living the same Christianity as always.

Several times my younger sister asked me to return to my city, because there it would be easier for me to get a job and I would no longer be in need, but even though I was hungry and having the war and the humiliation and mistreatment that my wife did to me, I answered her. several times to my sister "For these few I was left"

In the end they also left and I was alone and someone told me that he confronted one of them and said "You are quite ungrateful to that man and after he went through so much need for you" that person told us that the response he received was "We didn't ask him to make all that sacrifice for us"

I came to this city wanting to serve God, in the process I discovered that I was not even a Christian, that I did not even know the true gospel and finally that people are not going to change if they do not want to change.

I'm still in need, I'm still praying for my family and I'm still praying for what God can do with me and I actually feel like George Whitefield rowing that boat, waiting for God's miracle.

CHAPTER 14
Final Words.

First of all, I apologize to the people who read the first edition and found such a large number of errors. It was very painful for me to write this book of memoirs, or, rather, summary of memoirs, and I only did a personal revision as a bird's eye view of the previous version and then I ran it through an online proofreader and I felt confident that I was going to fix it. everything, but it was not like that.

At this moment, since I feel better emotionally, I can do an almost complete review of the book, I only missed chapter 13, which I hope has the fewest errors. And I pray to God that in general this second edition there are very few errors that the reader finds. And as retribution after this chapter, I have added photographic annexes to give credibility to the truths that I tell in this book and that will also be added to the audiobook version that I am "cooking" since my idea is that this book is in all versions and possible languages in order to prevent others from the suffering that I went through.

It is my hope that these memoirs can serve as a warning and as a teaching to each pastor and leader on how to behave and how to lead the flock for which one day they will have to give an account before the prince of shepherds.

I know by heart all the manipulations that pastors do to get you to have blind obedience to them, but my beloved, my beloved, if you love your pastor and you love yourself, the worst thing you can do is have blind obedience to him. They couldn't manipulate me personally by telling me that if I didn't prostrate myself before the man of God, something bad was going to happen to me because my life was always horrible, but there are people who are afraid of that and I believe that the devil contributes by making Things happen to you when you doubt something that "The Man of God" did or said, then you begin to believe that those curses are true.

I never intend with what I write that you disrespect your pastor, love him, respect him and give him the honor he deserves, but please be careful with that fine line between honor and idolatry.

Please pray for your pastor, but in the right way, don't just pray for him for blessing or for God to remove everyone who is against him, in many cases the one who is against him is himself.

And if you who are reading this book are a pastor's wife, please be careful of his emotional shortcomings, look at what happened to my mother and even the mistakes that I myself made due to the need for affection. My mother had never received the affection that woman "X" showed her, much less woman "Y" and look at everything that caused that.

You know, Mrs. Pastor's wife, in the midst of us children not understanding how my father did so many bad things to us children and "God" continued to use him, the answer my mother gave us was "Sometimes one has to pay a price." for the call of another" That is, we paid the price of his call by enduring bad treatment. Don't do that, Mrs. Pastor's Wife. At another time my mother said that in the end the children leave and the husband is left, that's why she dedicated herself more to supporting him than to defending us from his mistreatment. Today he is the one who left.

I think this book is not only useful for pastors, pastors' wives and leaders but for any church member. Today while I was doing the spelling checks, I remembered how my father taught the church that even if they saw him doing something bad they couldn't say anything to him because he was the one who was going to give an account to God and my father once told me to my face that this is how I If I saw that something he did was wrong, I had to say it was right because he was the pastor.

I heard all kinds of preachings about the supposed curses that come to people for talking about the man of God and normally people are so afraid of that that the congregation ends up becoming a sect. Beloved, we must understand that all of this is manipulation.

I know people who are still afraid to talk about horrible things they saw their pastors do for fear of curses. I have not wanted to describe in this book all the forms of manipulation that I saw my mother, my father and other pastors practice because of my concern that this book will be seen as a way of attacking people or ministries, and I am already thinking that the Trying not to think of me in the wrong way could be omitting important things. If I come to that conclusion, when this book is published, I commit to writing another book describing all the types of manipulation these people use.

Let us also understand that these types of pastors appear to be very humble and sincere, but the truth is that they are deceivers and manipulators.

There is so much to learn in this book, that if you see it with the eyes and hearts for whom I wrote it, you can get a lot of benefit from it and it is my plea that it be so.

I want to repeat once again that no, I have nothing against my parents. With this book I do not intend to harm you but to help the bride of Christ. I pray every day for my parents, because I know that in the situation they are in, if they die or Christ comes, they will be lost. For this reason, sometimes I don't even sleep at night praying for them, sometimes I get up at dawn just to pray for my family.

To finish, I want to recommend a book that was a blessing to understand all this, the book is called: "An Emotionally Healthy Church" by Peter Scazzero, in this book there is a reflection on the reasons why men with gifts and abilities whom we call "men of God" have skeletons in their closets and present how leaders can prevent these things from happening. If you can't find this book you can go to the library: https://librosquevalelapenaleer.blogspot.com/ I assure you it is there, remember to buy this book to support your writer and buy my other books please, I know they will be a blessing to you and also all my books are related to each other.

If this book has been a blessing to you, please purchase it and give it to your pastor, pastor's wife, or a leader you love. Maybe it is not happening to you, but it can be a vaccine so that it never happens to you, because if you take the teachings that this book intends to teach you, you cannot imagine how many lives you will be helping to change. Kisses, I am Alias Martín García. epbaliasmartingarcia@gmail.com

Annexes

87

Since I am not given to lying, I would like to add some photos that attest to several things I say in the book.

The Beginnings of the Church.

A reminder to this day

Building the Church where the Workshop

2006/11/25 6:28 am

Construction

This was the photo that a brother from the church published a few days after my mother told me that they were going to think carefully before entering another ministry so quickly. They already had the logo and the name of the ministry on the pulpit.

The photo below means a lot to me. And it has a very painful story that does not appear in the e-book or the audiobook. The reason why this photo means so much is that when I wanted to study after high school there were no ways and some brothers from the church offered to help me but my father began to wage war on them saying that they were supporting a weakling, in the end the brothers They gave in to pressure and did not continue paying for my school fees.

When at the institute they did not allow me to register for the next semester because of the debts I had there, I cried like a child because I love studying. I always say that if I had had the manners, I would already have like 100 specializations. The saddest thing about this is that my father, having to help me, did not do it.

11 years later when I was able to complete my studies and graduate, I came home and took a

photo of it. I think that if one day someone offered to buy me that ugly, poor-quality photo, I would say: "That photo is priceless."

This is the witness of my sadness but also of my Joy.

Me doing what I love.

Me in the city where I am living with the
group that remained after most of them
left

If we decided to practice humility and get rid of all pride and not worry about what people might think of us but rather what God might think about us, there would be no skeletons in the closets.

I have taken many lessons from everything I described in the book. One of them is to recognize my sins and ask for forgiveness. At the time of publishing this audio book, my parents are still fighting so that no one finds out about their skeletons, because they are worried about what people will think about them. This reminds me a lot of Saul who only cared about what the people thought of him. It is my prayer that you will not be another Saul.

Let people think what they think, the important thing is that we are right with God.

Also by Alias Martín Garcia

SKELETONS IN THE CLOSET: Memories of a Son of a Pastor
Esqueletos en el Closet - Memorias de un hijo de Pastor - 2da Edición
Skeletons in the Closet - Memoirs of a Pastor's Son - 2nd Edition